What's Awake?

Rats

Patricia Whitehouse

KU-723-424

Raintree

www.raintreepublishers.co.uk
Visit our website to find out
more information about
Raintree books.

To order:
☎ Phone +44 (0) 1865 888066
🖹 Fax +44 (0) 1865 314091
🖳 Visit www.raintreepublishers.co.uk

Raintree is an imprint of Capstone Global Library
Limited, a company incorporated in England and Wales having
its registered office at 7 Pilgrim Street, London, EC4V 6LB
- Registered company number: 6695582

"Raintree" is a registered trademark of Pearson Education
Limited, under licence to Capstone Global Library Limited

Text © Capstone Global Library Limited 2003, 2010
Second edition first published in hardback and paperback
  in 2010
The moral rights of the proprietor have been asserted.

All rights reserved. No part of this publication may be
reproduced in any form or by any means (including
photocopying or storing it in any medium by electronic means
and whether or not transiently or incidentally to some other
use of this publication) without the written permission of the
copyright owner, except in accordance with the provisions
of the Copyright, Designs and Patents Act 1988 or under the
terms of a licence issued by the Copyright Licensing Agency,
Saffron House, 6–10 Kirby Street, London EC1N 8TS (www.
cla.co.uk). Applications for the copyright owner's written
permission should be addressed to the publisher.

Edited by Adrian Vigliano and Diyan Leake
Designed by Joanna Hinton-Malivoire
Picture research by Tracy Cummins
Originated by Chroma Graphics (Overseas) Pte Ltd
Printed in China by South China Printing
  Company Ltd

ISBN 978 1 4062 1238 9 (hardback)
14 13 12 11 10
10 9 8 7 6 5 4 3 2 1

ISBN 978 1 4062 1243 3 (paperback)
14 13 12 11 10
10 9 8 7 6 5 4 3 2 1

British Library Cataloguing in Publication Data
Whitehouse, Patricia, 1958-
  Rats. - 2nd ed. - (What's awake?)
  1. Rats - Juvenile literature 2. Nocturnal animals -
Juvenile literature
  I. Title
  599.3'5

Acknowledgements
We would like to thank the following for permission to
reproduce photographs: Alamy p. 21 (© VWPICS/J. M.
Labat); Animals Animals p. 18 (© Stouffer Prod.); Ardea p.
22 (© Jean Michel Labat); Getty Images pp. 5 (© James L.
Stanfield), 8 (© Joe McDonald), 14 (© Andrew Home), 16 (©
David J. Sams); istockphoto pp. 13 (© Ben Thomas), 20 (©
Roger Whiteway), 23d (© Peta Curnow); Minden Picture p.
15 (© Michael Durham); Photolibrary pp. 7 (© E.A. Janes),
10 (© Juniors Bildarchiv), 11 (© Gerhard Schulz); Photoshot
pp. 12 (© NHPA/Janes), 19 (© NHPA/Joe Blossom); Photo
Researchers p. 17 (© Tom McHugh); Shutterstock pp. 4 (©
Lloyd Smith), 6 (© Alexander Lukin), 9 (© Adam J. Sablich),
23a (© Bruce MacQueen), 23b (© Oleksii Abramov), 23c (©
Martin Wall), 23e (© Devin Koob).

Cover photograph of a rat reproduced with permission of
Minden Pictures (© Michael Durham). Back cover photograph
of a rat's snout reproduced with permission of istockphoto (©
Peta Curnow) and photograph of a rat's tail reproduced with
permission of istockphoto (© Roger Whiteway).

Every effort has been made to contact copyright holders
of material reproduced in this book. Any omissions will
be rectified in subsequent printings if notice is given to
the publisher.

 CAUTION: Remind children that it is not a good idea to handle wild animals.
Children should wash their hands with soap and water after they touch any animal.

Contents

What's awake? 4

What are rats? 6

What do rats look like? 8

Where do rats live? 10

What do rats do at night? 12

What do rats eat? 14

What do rats sound like? 16

How are rats special? 18

Where do rats go during the day? . . .20

Rat map 22

Picture glossary 23

Index 24

Some words are shown in bold, **like this**. You can find them in the picture glossary on page 23.

What's awake?

Some animals are awake when you go to sleep.

Animals that stay awake at night are **nocturnal**.

Rats are awake at night.

What are rats?

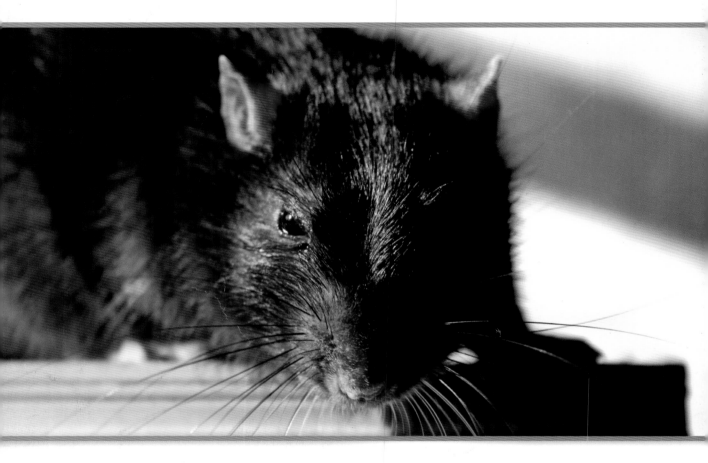

Rats are mammals.

Mammals have **fur** on their bodies.

Mammals live with their babies.

Mammals make milk for their babies.

What do rats look like?

tail

snout

Rats look like big mice with long tails.

They have dark eyes and pointed **snouts**.

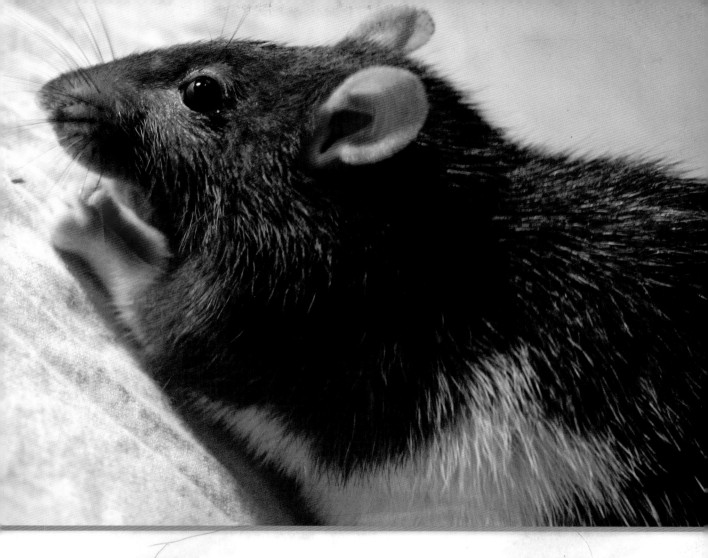

A rat's **fur** can be brown or black.

It can be grey or white.

Where do rats live?

Rats live together in **nests**.

In towns and cities, some rats live in underground pipes.

Some rats live in old buildings.

In the wild, they live in trees
or underground.

What do rats do at night?

Rats wake up after dark.

They leave their **nest**.

Rats look for food.

They can eat all night.

What do rats eat?

Rats eat almost anything.

In the wild, rats eat birds' eggs, insects, and plants.

In towns and cities, rats eat these things, too.

They also eat food from rubbish bins, and pet food that people leave out.

What do rats sound like?

Rats can squeak and whistle.

They can also make a chirping noise.

How are rats special?

Rats' teeth are very strong.

This rat is chewing on an **antler**.

Rats' front teeth do not
stop growing.

They chew things to keep their
teeth short.

Where do rats go during the day?

Rats go back to their **nests** during the day.

They may also look for food during the day.

They take care of their babies.

Then they sleep for most of the day.

Rat map

snout

tail

Picture glossary

 **antler** hard part that some animals have growing on their head

 **fur** soft hair that some animals have on their bodies

 **nest** place where birds and some kinds of other animals live and have their family

 **nocturnal** awake at night

 **snout** long nose and mouth that some animals have

Index

babies 7, 21

eyes 8

food 13, 15, 20

fur 6, 9

mammals 6, 7

milk 7

nests 10, 12, 20

noises 17

snouts 8, 22

tails 8, 22

teeth 18, 19

Note to parents and teachers

Reading for information is an important part of a child's literacy development. Learning begins with a question about something. Help the children think of themselves as investigators and researchers by encouraging their questions about the world around them. In this book, the animal is identified as a mammal. A mammal by definition is one that is covered with hair or fur, and feeds its young with milk from its body. Point out the fact that, although the animal in this book is a mammal, many other animals are mammals – including humans.